Copyright © 2020 Justin Rossow and Nex

ISBN: 9798640894875 · Imprint: Independently published

Cover design: Brett Jordan, bit.ly/brett_blog

Cover image: Elisa Schulz, www.elisaschulzphotography.com

Typefaces: Montserrat & Raleway

Special thanks to Ellen Davis for copy editing, to Elisa Schulz for the cover photo, and to Brett Jordan for cover design work.

I am grateful to Brendan Knorp for music layout and Linda Ekong for internal layout.

Lead Illustrator Valerie Matyas and the gifted artists from Visual Faith Ministry are a joy to work with. I am thankful that they help me know and follow Jesus.

We want to help resource your congregation or small group. Templates of the INRI Prayer and the Big Rocks Prayer are found on pages 128-129 of this book for you to copy and use.

If you would like to reproduce any other pages, please email Innovation@FindMyNextStep.org to receive permission. The illustrations belong to the artists. We want you to be able to use these illustrations to help people delight in taking a next step following Jesus. In order to use them, you need express permission from Next Step Press, which we are glad to give.

Let's talk.

www.findmynextstep.org

Ponder Anew
A Hymn Journal of Trust & Confidence

Introduction: Hymn Journal Theology

A hymn journal combines music, art, and Scripture as a way of engaging God's Word. But what's actually happening *theologically* when you sketch, doodle, draw, add color, collage, and sing along?

The Scriptures actually talk about how we engage Scripture. And when God's Word talks about handling God's Word, we get a wide variety of metaphors. Some of the richest imagery for handling the Word of God shows up in the Psalms.

Psalm 1 for example, talks about the person whose "delight is in the *Torah* of Yahweh" or the "*Law* of the Lord." The context makes clear we're not just talking "rules" here; *Torah* in this case is the whole story of creation and redemption and promise of more to come.

And the blessed person who delights in this divine Story? That person "meditates" on this Word of God "day and night." You could translate "meditate" in this verse as "chew"; the vocab can refer to *how a cow chews and rechews its cud* all day long.

Or you might want to go with the word's other core meaning here: *to crush an herb and release its aroma, flavor, and power.* Imagine taking a handful of fresh lemon basil or chocolate mint and grinding it between your hands and taking a deep breath.

MINT

sage

OREGANO

THYME

aroma

DILL

power

flavor

That pungent bouquet is like Scripture: God's Word has power of and by itself, always and everywhere; and when you handle God's Word, you release that universal power into your own personal space and experience.

Take another of my favorites: you know Psalm 119 talks about God's Word as "a lamp to my feet and a light for my path" (verse 105), but did you know that one of the many words Psalm 119 uses for "meditating" on the Word is a verb that basically means "*to play*?"

It's the same Hebrew vocabulary word we get in Isaiah 11:8.

> *The infant will play [sha'a'] near the cobra's den, and the young child will put its hand into the viper's nest.* (Isaiah 11:8, NIV)

That "play" word describes the kind of delight you get from just having fun:

- coasting down a big hill on a bike;
- swinging on a tire swing;
- taking a running leap off the dock;
- grabbing the front seat on a roller coaster.

Anything that makes you go, "Whee!!" and then bust out laughing is probably a pretty good approximation of the Hebrew word *sha'a'*. It's even fun to say: "*Shah-AH!*"

Notice how that playful delight shows up again and again throughout Psalm 119:

> *I will delight [sha'a'] in your statutes;*
> *I will not forget your word ...*
>
> *I find delight [sha'a'] in your commandments, which I love ...*
>
> *Let your mercy come to me, that I may live; for your law is my delight [sha'a'] ...*
>
> *If your law had not been my delight [sha'a'], I would have perished in my affliction.*
>
> (Psalm 119:16, 47, 77, 92, ESV)

Psalm 119 seems to think we should take playful delight in God's Word. That play/sport/delight vocabulary word can be translated as "meditating" on God's Word: not just *thinking* about it intellectually, but *playing* with it; *exploring* it; handling the Word of Truth so that its eternal significance also has meaning for me, today (and *having fun* doing it).

The purpose of "meditating" on the Word—crushing the herbs, finding playful delight in the text—the purpose of handling Scriptures is to plant that Word deep in your heart so it can grow and bear fruit. That's what I see going on with hymn journaling.

Music can *glorify God* all by itself; and music can also *deliver the Word*.

Art can also glorify God just by being Art, and if you spend any time on Pinterest or Facebook, you'll see people talking about how Bible journaling is a kind of worship that brings glory to God.

I think that's right, but not yet complete. Art can *glorify God*, but more than that, Art can *also deliver the Word*; I think that's where the true power (and real fun) comes in.

Take this comment from one of the people who engaged our first hymn journal (*When from Death I'm Free: A Hymn Journal for Holy Week*):

"I'm amazed by the double dose of concentration and devotion that music and visual meditation is allowing me. I walk around the house humming the melody, recalling the images, and repeating the lyrics. It is really quite powerful."

Did you get that? The music delivers the Word. The visual imagery delivers the Word. The Word is powerful and active in your daily life, on your lips and in your heart, as you walk around the house.

Another Facebook member posted: *"I'm loving how the artwork makes me take more time on my devotion and really ponder and pray. I especially like the visual faith experiments."*

Taking more time—that's like rubbing the herb (or chewing the cud...). An "experiment" tied to "visual faith"—that's got *sha'a'* written all over it, taking playful delight in engaging the Word.

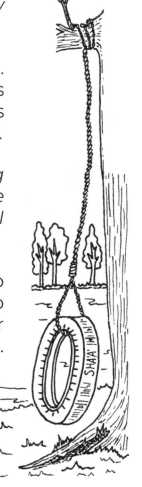

St. Augustine famously said, "The one who sings, prays twice." I'd like to add, "And the one who draws, or colors, or sketches, or doodles, prays again and again and again."

The power is already there in the Word. Handling the Word (along with the colored pencils and markers and gel pens and Washi tape) brings the power of the Word to bear in your day, in your week, in your life.

And where the Word is present in your life, you can trust Jesus is present, too. Jesus is the Word of God who got His hands dirty for us; now that same Jesus is present by His Spirit as we get our hands dirty in the Word. The result is a powerful aroma that stays with you all day.

Oh, and *fun*; don't forget the pure delight of having Scripture stains on your fingers and in your heart as you go about your daily routine.

The theology of a hymn journal is tied directly to the theology of the Word of God, the Word who became flesh and dwelt among us so He could be seen and handled and touched.

God's Word still comes to us. The Spirit still opens the Scriptures and makes our hearts burn. Jesus is still present whenever and however the Word is delivered. That's what a hymn journal is all about.

But the proof is in the pudding. *Bon appétit!*

Justin Rossow, Next Step Press

How to Use This Book

Consider this hymn journal one giant opportunity—a huge, low-pressure, high-reward opportunity—to try, to experiment, to dig in and absorb the Word of God through music, art, and the written word.

There is no right or wrong way to use this resource. But here are a few ideas to get you started.

1. Make This Book Your Own

This is your book. You can write in it, draw in it, paint it, tear it, cut out a page, or tape something right in the middle of it. I encourage you to use, personalize, modify, and make it work for you and for your life today. Consider writing your name inside the front cover as a reminder that this is your space to play and experiment. You'll get something right, and you'll get something else wrong, and who cares? It's yours to use as you will. No pressure. No stress.

2. Create a Permissions Page

Children rarely need permission to experiment with doodling or underlining or adding color or writing in the margins; we adults often do.

In the blank space headed by the initials "JJ," below, create a "permissions page." ("JJ" stands for "Jesu, Juva" or "Jesus, help!") Use that, or any other prayer, to dedicate your time in this journal to God's glory and to whatever the Spirit wants to do in your life. Add your name, the date, and a favorite Bible verse to your prayer of dedication. You now have permission to go out on a limb; Jesus will meet you there.

3. Dig Into the Word

Read the Scripture verses in each chapter. Then read them again. Then read them out loud. Circle, star, underline, or highlight single words and phrases that grab your attention. Draw arrows to connect repeated thoughts in different verses. Jot notes in the margin. Look up parallel passages and record them on the page. Dig into the Word; be willing to get your hands dirty.

Try the same with the hymns. Find an online musical recording. Sing along. Listen to two or three other versions. On the hymn page, circle or add color to words or phrases that are meaningful to you. Watch for repeating thoughts. Doodle in the margins. Draw liturgical symbols or add Bible references. If you can read music, plunk out the melody line. Less musically inclined? Recite the lyrics as a poem.

Dig into the words: the readings, the hymns, and the devotions. The more meaningful ways you engage and layer the Word, the more you will take that Word with you into your day and week.

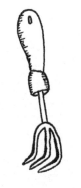

4. Add Color

I mean add lots and lots of color. You don't have to consider yourself artistic or have a stash of supplies to make this journal meaningful. Use whatever is readily available: crayons, markers, colored pencils, watercolors, and gel pens can all do the trick. Try stickers, stamps, stencils, or tracing.

Experiment with magazine clippings and Washi tape (or Scotch tape, or even duct tape!) to create a mixed media collage. Use your favorite pen to record thoughts, ideas, new insights, concrete promises, and steadfast truths.

These illustrations were prayerfully created to lead you into a moment of prayerful engagement with the Word. As you add color or text, you are spending focused time in the presence of Jesus. The Holy Spirit promises to be active in the Word.

Pray as you sketch or color or paint or highlight. Let the process take precedence over the final product. Your goal is not museum art. Think of it more as "fridge art," the kind of art from loved ones that hangs on your refrigerator. As you offer your artwork to your Heavenly Father, God proudly puts it on heaven's fridge with a smile and thinks of you.

5. Fill in the Blanks
We left some pages of this hymn journal blank on purpose, in case your colors bleed through. (If you are using media like markers or paint, try using an inexpensive flexible cutting board under your work to protect the remaining pages.)

If you do experience color bleed, you have a couple of options. First, you could incorporate the colors from the bleed into its own creative design; add more lines, color, or a quotation to turn those random blobs of color into further opportunities for meditation.

Second, the bleed pages offer a great space for a "tip-in" or "tip-out"—a washi-taped addition of a worship bulletin, note card, illustrated margin, or mini collage. You could even glue a clean piece of white or decorative paper over the bleed to start fresh with something new.

If your colors don't bleed, then you are faced with one of the most frightening things in any creative endeavor: a blank page! Don't panic. You can try something different every time, or find something that works and repeat it on every blank page.

Try using that space to write out a letter to Jesus as a form of prayer. If you like sketching, create your own image to go with the chapter. If you like writing, add another verse or two to the hymn. If you are digitally creative, consider designing a onepage medley of images or definitions or Bible verses, print it out, and add it to your book. View the blank space as an opportunity, not an obstacle to your journey.

6. Reflect, Respond, Remember, Share
As you write and pray and sketch and circle and add color and engage the Word, make sure you also note what's going on in your life. Add dates to your prayer requests. Be concrete and specific. One of the benefits of a hymn journal like this one comes weeks, months, or even years after the fact.

We published our first hymn journal right before COVID-19 led to stay-at-home orders. Events were cancelled. Buildings, including churches, were closed. We went from a Lent where many of us were at church twice a week to worship in living rooms, eyes fixed on screens, thankful for livestreaming. And in the middle of all of that, we were reading and singing and adding color and prayer requests to a hymn journal for Holy Week.

If my future grandkids ever ask me about what that strange time was like, I will have a record of my prayers and struggles, of God's grace and mercy, of the comfort of Jesus and the fellowship of the Holy Spirit on the pages of my hymn journal. When you write or draw or paint or reflect or create colorful illustrations or collages, you are also recording in a concrete way what Jesus is doing in your life.

You can revisit these pages to remind yourself of the Scriptures and prayers that meant the most to you. You can share these pages, already now, with people you know and love. And years from now, when the specifics of this week and these troubles are long past, this testimony of God's faithfulness will still be a reminder that Jesus walked with you through it all.

You don't have to consider yourself particularly creative to use this book. And you may be surprised what the Holy Spirit will do as you try new ways of engaging the Word. Blessings on the journey.

Valerie E. Matyas, Visual Faith Ministry

JJ

1. Praise to the Lord, the Almighty

Author: Joachim Neander
Translator: Catherine Winkworth

Text and tune:
Public domain

1. Praise to the Lord, the Almighty, the King of creation! O my soul, praise Him, for He is your health and salvation! Let all who hear Now to His temple draw near, Joining in glad adoration!

2. Praise to the Lord, who o'er all things is wondrously reigning And, as on wings of an eagle, uplifting, sustaining. Have you not seen All that is needful has been Sent by His gracious ordaining?

3. Praise to the Lord, who has fearfully, wondrously, made you; Health has bestowed and, when heedlessly falling, has stayed you. What need or grief ever has failed of relief? Wings of His mercy did shade you.

4. Praise to the Lord, who will prosper your work and defend you; Surely His goodness and mercy shall daily attend you. Ponder anew What the Almighty can do As with His love he befriends you.

5. Praise to the Lord! Oh, let all that is in us adore Him! All that has life and breath, come now with praises before Him! Let the amen Sound from His people again. Gladly forever adore Him!

John 15:9-17 (NIV)

As the Father has loved me, so have I loved you.
Now remain in my love.

If you keep my commands,
you will remain in my love,
just as I have kept my Father's commands
and remain in his love.

I have told you this so that my joy may be in
you and that your joy may be complete.

My command is this:
Love each other as I have loved you.

Greater love has no one than this:
to lay down one's life for one's friends.

You are my friends if you do what I command.
I no longer call you servants, because a
servant does not know his master's business.

Instead, I have called you friends,
for everything that I learned from my Father
I have made known to you.

You did not choose me,
but I chose you and appointed you
so that you might go and bear fruit—
fruit that will last—and so that whatever you
ask in my name the Father will give you.

This is my command: Love each other.

Ponder Anew

I love spending time with my best friend. Sometimes we just hang out: play a game, share some stories, have a beer. Sometimes the conversation is more serious: what I'm struggling with, what made me confused, what broke my heart.

I can entrust my friend with who I really am, how I really feel, and what I really think, even if I am not sure what that is; even if I don't like what that is.

I have learned, over time, that I can trust my friend to listen, to encourage, to laugh, to console, to forgive, to share my life, my dreams, my sorrow, my hopes, my failure, my shame, my hurt—me; all of me; the unfiltered me.

If you try to make Jesus your buddy or God your BFF, of course you will miss some of the most important things about God's transcendence and power and perfection and regal power. At the same time, God actually called Abraham, "Friend." Jesus actually called His disciples, "Friends."

Your relationship with the Almighty God, King of the Universe, majestic in power and glory from eternity and to eternity, is so much more than the relationship you have even with your closest friend.

But your relationship with God is never less than that. Jesus is not just Lord and King; Jesus is your friend; your closest friend; your most trusted friend.

Ponder anew what the *Almighty* can do, as with His love He *befriends* you.

Praise to the Lord, the Almighty,
the King of creation!
O my soul, praise Him,
for He is your health and salvation!
   Let all who hear
      now to His temple draw near,
      joining in glad adoration!

Praise to the Lord, who o'er all things
is wondrously reigning
and, as on wings of an eagle,
uplifting, sustaining.
   Have you not seen
      all that is needful has been
      sent by His gracious ordaining?

Praise to the Lord, who has fearfully,
wondrously, made you;
health has bestowed and, when
heedlessly falling, has stayed you.
   What need or grief
      ever has failed of relief?
      Wings of His mercy did shade you.

Praise to the Lord, who will
prosper your work and defend you;
surely His goodness and mercy
shall daily attend you.
    Ponder anew
        what the Almighty can do
        as with His love He befriends you.

Praise to the Lord!
Oh let all that is in us adore Him!
All that has life and breath,
come now with praises before Him!
    Let the Amen
        sound from His people again;
        gladly forever adore him!

Faith Experiment: My Friend, Jesus

Jesus calls us "friends." Of course, Jesus is more than our best buddy; still, Jesus uses friendship as one lens through which He wants us to view our relationship with Him. As the Almighty God called Abraham "friend," and Abraham believed the Lord, now Jesus calls you friend and invites you to trust that invitation.

Our relationship to Jesus is much more than human friendship; but it is not less than human friendship. Looking at your relationship with your friends can give you a new way to see your relationship with God.

Begin by thinking of some of the best human friendships you have ever experienced. What things have you liked most about your best friends? What brought you joy and comfort and strength in your relationship? On a very practical level, how did you spend your time when you got together with your best friends?

After you have filled out the two left-hand boxes on the next page, ponder anew your relationship with Jesus. How do your *friends* help you see in a new way the things you like most about *Jesus*? How do the activities that build *friendships* over time translate to *your relationship with God*?

What attitudes or actions might you add or remove from your faith walk as you share life with Jesus? Ponder anew, what the Almighty can do, as with His love He befriends you.

MY FRIENDS

JESUS

What I Like Most About MY BEST FRIENDS

BEST

What I Like Most About JESUS

How I Spend Time With MY BEST FRIENDS

TICKET

How I Spend Time With JESUS

PONDER ANEW

2. What a Friend We Have in Jesus

Text: Joseph Scriven
Tune: Charles Converse

Text and Tune:
Public Domain

1. What a friend we have in Je - sus, All our sins and griefs to bear!
2. Have we tri - als and temp - ta - tions? Is there trou - ble an - y - where?
3. Are we weak and heav - y lad - en, Cum - bered with a load of care?

What a priv - i - lege to car - ry Ev - 'ry-thing to God in prayer!
We should nev - er be dis - cour-aged; Take it to the Lord in prayer.
Pre - cious Sav-ior, still our ref - uge Take it to the Lord in prayer.

Oh what peace we of - ten for - feit, Oh what need-less pain we bear,
Can we find a friend so faith - ful. Who will all our sor - rows share?
Do your friends de-spise, for-sake you? Take it to the Lord in prayer!

All be - cause we do not car - ry Ev - 'ry-thing to God in prayer!
Je - sus knows our ev - 'ry weak - ness; Take it to the Lord in prayer.
In His arms he'll take and shield you; You will find a sol - ace there.

WHAT a FRIEND we have in JESUS

All our sins & griefs to bear

Take it to the Lord in PRAYER

EF '20

1 Peter 5:6–11 (NIV)

Humble yourselves, therefore,
under God's mighty hand,
that he may lift you up in due time.

Cast all your anxiety on him
because he cares for you.

Be alert and of sober mind.
Your enemy the devil prowls around
like a roaring lion looking for someone to devour.
Resist him, standing firm in the faith,
because you know that the family of believers
throughout the world is undergoing
the same kind of sufferings.

And the God of all grace,
who called you to his eternal glory in Christ,
after you have suffered a little while,
will himself restore you
and make you strong, firm, and steadfast.

To him be the power for ever and ever. Amen.

Psalm 55:22 (ESV)

Cast your burden on the LORD,
and he will sustain you;
he will never permit the righteous to be moved.

All Our Sins and Griefs to Bear

Sometimes it's hard to lay down a burden, even if you are sick of carrying it.

I once met a woman who was carrying around rocks in her purse; six or seven stones about the size of a small egg.

On each she had written words, identity markers, hurtful things that her ex-husband had said to her during an ugly divorce. The stones said things like: "Ugly." "Stupid." "Fat." "Failure." Or worse.

Maybe writing those words gave some separation from the labels that wounded her so deeply. But not enough. When I met her, she had been carrying those rocks around every day, everywhere she went, for over a year. She hated them. She wanted to be rid of them. And she didn't know how to put the rocks down.

So in a dimly lit sanctuary, we approached God's presence together. We prayerfully committed her burden to the hands and heart of Jesus. With trembling fingers, she placed those stones on the altar, and left them there. She walked out of the building with her head held high, as if a heavy weight had been lifted.

What burden have you been carrying around lately? Are you afraid to let it go? Or, after all this time, have you forgotten how to set it down?

Trust Jesus. His hands can hold what is too heavy for you to carry. You don't need special permission or a perfect prayer to make it work.

Place your burden in the loving hands of Jesus; then open your hands and let go.

Take it to the Lord in PRAYER

What a friend we have in Jesus,
all our sins and griefs to bear!
What a privilege to carry
everything to God in prayer!

Oh what peace we often forfeit,
Oh what needless pain we bear,
all because we do not carry
everything to God in prayer!

Have we trials and temptations?
Is there trouble anywhere?
We should never be discouraged;
take it to the Lord in prayer!

Can we find a friend so faithful
who will all our sorrows share?
Jesus knows our every weakness;
take it to the Lord in prayer!

Are we weak and heavy laden,
cumbered with a load of care?
Precious Savior, still our refuge—
take it to the Lord in prayer!

Do your friends despise, forsake you?
Take it to the Lord in prayer!
In his arms He'll take and shield you;
you will find a solace there.

Prayer Experiment: The Big Rocks Prayer

You've probably seen the illustration before: begin with an empty jar or bucket. Fill it with small rocks and gravel, and then try to add some large rocks after the fact. It doesn't work so well.

The big, heavy, and important things have to go into your bucket first if you want to get them in at all. Then you can add the rest.

Prayer can be like that. We can spend all of our time in prayer on a long list and find, when it's time to say amen, we never really brought up the big, heavy, and important stuff. There just wasn't time.

Experiment with the Big Rocks Prayer on the following page and see if it helps you spend more time on the things that need the most attention.

Add prayer requests to the large rocks first. Then add smaller concerns to the smaller rocks. Anything else can be prayed about another time.

Pray as you color in the rocks, beginning with the biggest ones and working your way down. You have room to add words to the largest of the rocks if you wish; let the label be enough for the smaller rocks.

Once you have finished coloring the rocks, use a pen or marker or pencil to add "sand," tiny dots that fill the space between the rocks. Keep praying. Finally, use blue to cover the whole thing in "water" as you pray for the Spirit to cover your prayers. Your bucket is full. And Jesus now carries your rocks, big and small. You can leave them in His hands. Be at peace.

3. Great is Thy Faithfulness

Text: Thomas Chisholm
Tune: William Runyan

Text and Tune:
Public Domain

1. Great is Thy faith - ful-ness, O God my Fa - ther;
2. Sum - mer and win - ter and spring-time and har - vest,
3. Par - don for sin and a peace that en - dur - eth,

There is no sha - dow of turn - ing with Thee;
Sun, moon, and stars in their cours - es a - bove
Thine own dear pres - ence to cheer and to guide,

Thou chang - est not, Thy com - pas - sions, they fail not;
Join with all na - ture in man - i - fold wit - ness
strength for to - day and bright hope for to - mor - row,

As Thou hast been Thou for - ev - er wilt be.
To Thy great faith - ful - ness, mer - cy, and love.
Bless - ings all mine, with ten thou - sand be - side!

Great is Thy faith - ful-ness! Great is Thy faith - ful-ness!

Morn - ing by morn - ing new mer - cies I see:

All I have need - ed Thy hand hath pro - vid - ed

Great is Thy faith - ful-ness, Lord, un - to me!

morning by morning NEW MERCIES I SEE

All I have needed THY HAND HATH PROVIDED

Great is thy FAITHFULNESS

EA '20

Lamentations 3:19–26 (NIV)

I remember my affliction and my wandering,
the bitterness and the gall.

I well remember them,
and my soul is downcast within me.

Yet this I call to mind
and therefore I have hope:
because of the LORD's great love
we are not consumed,
for his compassions never fail.
They are new every morning;

great is your faithfulness.

I say to myself,
"TheLORD is my portion;
therefore I will wait for him."

The LORD is good
to those whose hope is in him,
to the one who seeks him;
it is good
to wait quietly
for the salvation of the LORD.

No Shadow of Turning in Thee

Change is everywhere. And change can be exhausting.

I look around me, and all I see is change. My job changes, my family changes, my daily routines change, my relationships change.

I look inside myself and all I see is change. My expectations change, my feelings change, my hopes, my plans, my memories, my goals, my sense of identity and purpose and peace—everything that makes me *me* is subject to whim, and chance, and entropy, and decay.

I have counted on other people, and been crushed by their sin and failure. I have counted on myself, and been equally devastated by my own sin and failure. Everywhere I look, inside and out, I find shifting sand.

The immutable, eternal, unchanging God stepped into human flesh and human *change*. Jesus made Himself susceptible to the whims of sinful people, to the failure of friends, to the entropy of death.

Jesus entered into human change because His heart stays the same. From the foundation of the world, Jesus has not wavered in His love for me. My sin can't change Jesus. My change of heart can't chase Jesus off. My failure can't turn Jesus aside.

Jesus is passionately and compassionately faithful: His faithfulness cannot change. Thanks be to God.

THERE IS NO SHADOW

OF TURNING WITH THEE

THOU CHANGEST NOT

THY COMPASSIONS THEY FAIL NOT

Great is Thy faithfulness, O God my Father;
there is no shadow of turning with Thee;
Thou changest not, Thy compassions, they fail not;
as Thou hast been Thou forever wilt be.

Great is Thy faithfulness! Great is Thy faithfulness!
Morning by morning new mercies I see:
all I have needed Thy hand hath provided--
Great is Thy faithfulness, Lord, unto me!

Summer and winter and springtime and
harvest,sun, moon, and stars in their courses above
join with all nature in manifold witness
to Thy great faithfulness, mercy, and love.

Great is Thy faithfulness! Great is Thy faithfulness!
Morning by morning new mercies I see:
all I have needed Thy hand hath provided--
Great is Thy faithfulness, Lord, unto me!

Pardon for sin and a peace that endureth,
Thine own dear presence to cheer and to guide,
strength for today and bright hope for tomorrow,
blessings all mine, with ten thousand beside!

Great is Thy faithfulness! Great is Thy faithfulness!
Morning by morning new mercies I see:
all I have needed Thy hand hath provided--
Great is Thy faithfulness, Lord, unto me!

Prayer Experiment: Seasons of Change

We know God is faithful in the midst of our seasons of change. In fact, the faithful rhythm of the seasons, even the ebb and flow of day and night, reflect God's faithfulness to us.

The four seasons are represented on the next page, but the scene needs your help. Add buds or flowers to the Spring Tree on the upper left. Talk to Jesus about the things He is planting in your life right now. Write down a few of those things in the branches as you color the scene.

Then dress the tree in the upper right with the full green of summertime. Talk to Jesus about the things that are alive and well and bursting with life in your experience right now. Jot down a few thoughts on or around your Summer Tree.

The Autumn Tree on the bottom right needs you to add fall colors and maybe some ripe fruit. What things in your life are bearing fruit right now? How do you see the results of your time and labor? Add a few notes and talk to Jesus about where He is seeing you bear fruit or inviting you to bear fruit.

Finally, leave the branches of the Winter Tree in the bottom left barren. Add a winter scene around the tree and wonder with Jesus about things He is intentionally leaving fallow in your life right now. What areas of your life are resting in this season? Where is the Father lovingly pruning you? What in your life are you letting go of right now? Add your thoughts to the Winter Tree and hold all four seasons before Jesus in prayer.

THOU
CHANGEST
NOT

For I
the LORD
do not change.
—Malachi 6:3

4. How Firm a Foundation

Text: Unknown
Tune: Unknown

Text and Tune:
Public Domain

1. How firm a foun-da-tion, O saints of the Lord,
2. "Fear not, I am with you, Oh be not dis-mayed,
3. "When through ery tri-als your path-way will lie,
4. "Through-out all their life-time my peo-ple will prove

Is laid for your faith in His ex-cel-lent Word!
For I am your God and will still give you aid;
My grace, all-suf-fi-cient, will be your sup-ply.
My sov-'reign, e-ter-nal, un-change-a-ble love;

What more can He say than to you He has said Who
I'll strength-en you, help you, and cause you to stand, Up -
The flames will not hurt you; I on-ly de-sign Your
And then, when grey hairs will their tem-ples a-dorn, Like

un - to the Sav - ior for ref - uge have fled?
held by My righ - teous, om - nip - o - tent hand.
dross to con - sume and your gold to re - fine.
lambs they will still in My bo - som be borne."

Isaiah 43:1-4; 46:3-4 (ESV)

*But now thus says the L*ORD*,*
he who created you, O Jacob,
    he who formed you, O Israel:

"Fear not, for I have redeemed you;
    I have called you by name, you are mine.

When you pass through the waters,
I will be with you; and through the rivers,
they shall not overwhelm you;
when you walk through fire you shall not be
burned, and the flame shall not consume you.

*For I am the L*ORD *your God,*
    the Holy One of Israel, your Savior.
I give Egypt as your ransom,
    Cush and Seba in exchange for you.

Because you are precious in my eyes,
    and honored, and I love you,
I give men in return for you,
    peoples in exchange for your life.

Listen to me, O house of Jacob,
all the remnant of the house of Israel,
who have been borne by me from before your
birth, carried from the womb;

even to your old age I am he,
    and to gray hairs I will carry you.
I have made, and I will bear;
    I will carry and will save.

Fear Not! I Am With You

It's amazing how *unreliable* life can be. On one day, you can find yourself neck deep in a river whose current threatens to sweep you off of your feet. The next, you are surrounded by fire that turns to ash things that once seemed so reliable. You face these extremes with little or no warning, and you never know what the next day will bring.

It's amazing, how *reliable* God can be. Pregnant women and nursing mothers carried infants through the Red Sea while God's Presence stood guard. Old priests who carried the Ark of the Covenant placed wrinkled feet into the raging Jordan River, and crossed on dry ground. Young men in their prime were thrown into a fiery furnace and came out unscathed because the Messenger of the Presence of Yahweh stood in the midst of the flames.

In Jesus, the very presence of the Almighty God goes with you into the raging deep. In Jesus, the Living God lifts you up and carries you securely, from before you were born, to the prime of your life, to your old age and gray hairs. Jesus, the Messenger of the Presence of Yahweh, stands next to you in the flames.

Following Jesus does not exempt you from fire and flood, confusion and loss; but in Jesus, you will never be alone.

FEAR NOT I AM

with you Always

ag 2020

How firm a foundation, O saints of the Lord,
Is laid for your faith in His excellent Word!
What more can He say than to you He has said
Who unto the Savior for refuge have fled?

"Fear not! I am with you, Oh be not dismayed,
For I am your God and will still give you aid;
I'll strengthen you, help you, and cause you to stand,
Upheld by My righteous, omnipotent hand.

"The soul that on Jesus has leaned for repose
I will not, I will not, desert to his foes;
That soul, though all hell should endeavor to shake,
I'll never, no never, no never forsake!

"When through fiery trials your pathway will lie,
My grace, all-sufficient, will be your supply.
The flames will not hurt you; I only design
Your dross to consume and your gold to refine.

"Throughout all their lifetime My people will prove
My sov'reign, eternal, unchangeable love;
And then, when gray hairs will their temples adorn,
Like lambs they will still in My bosom be borne."

Prayer Experiment: Bible Margins

Each of the three illustrations on the following page can be used in a variety of ways.

They are designed to fit in the margins of many study Bibles. You can lay a page of your Bible over your favorite illustration and copy it into your Bible. Then add color as you prayerfully meditate on the text. Margin art leaves a record in your Bible of the time you spent with God in prayer—a kind of "selfie with God" that captures your time together.

Or, you can use these illustrations as bookmarks. Cut them out of your book (or print them from our website onto thick paper). Then prayerfully color them in as you meditate on the text. When you are done, use them to mark your spot in your Bible or in any other book you are reading.

OR, you can use these illustrations as prayer cards: cut out (or print) at least one of each of these. Pray for someone in your life based on the text. Add a note of encouragement on the back, and when you are done, mail, text, or email the card to the person you prayed for. That physical reminder of your prayer will be an encouragement to your family and friends.

OR ... use the illustrations on the next page as a starting point for your own design. Prayerfully choose one of the verses from Isaiah 43 or 46 and illustrate those words. Run an experiment. How might you communicate the meaning of that verse in bookmark size? What style of letters would you use? What images are important to capture? When you've finished, do one or more of the suggestions above with your own Bible Margin art!

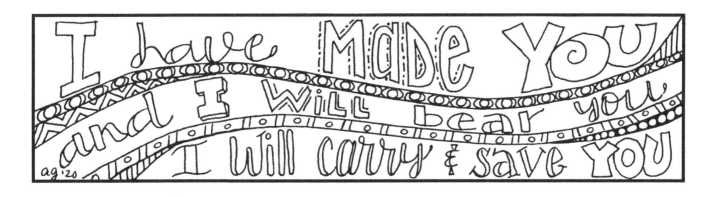

I have Made You and I Will bear you, I Will carry & save YOU

When You Walk Through Fire You Will Not Be Burned Isaiah 43:2

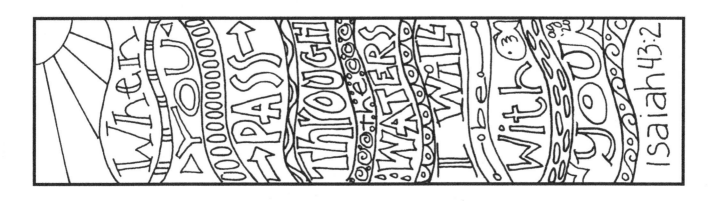

When You Pass Through the Waters I Will be With You Isaiah 43:2

Fear Not for I have Redeemed YOU Isaiah 43:1

5. O Love, How Deep, How Broad, How High!

Text: Thomas Kempis
Trans: Benjamin Webb

Text and Tune:
Public Domain

1. O love, how deep, how broad, how high,
2. He sent no an - gel to our race,
3. For us bap - tized, for us He bore
4. For us He prayed; for us He taught;
5. For us, by wick - ed - ness be - trayed,

Be - yond all thought and fan - ta - sy,
Of high - er or of low - er place,
His ho - ly fast and hunger - ed sore;
For us His dai - ly works He wrought,
For us, in crown of thorns ar - rayed,

That God, the Son of God, should take
But wore the robe of hu - man frame,
For us temp - ta - tion sharp He knew;
By words and signs and ac - tions thus
He bore the shame - ful cross and death;

Our mor - tal form for mor - tals' sake!
And to this world Him - self He came
For us the temp - ter ov - er - threw.
Still seek - ing not Him - self, but us.
For us, He gave His dy - ing breath.

6. For us He rose from death again;
for us He went on high to reign;
for us He sent His Spirit here
to guide, to strengthen, and to cheer.

7. All glory to our Lord and God
for love so deep, so high, so broad;
the Trinity whom we adore,
forever and forevermore.

44

Philippians 2:5–13 (ESV)
Though he was in the form of God,
[Jesus] did not count equality with God
a thing to be grasped, but emptied himself,
by taking the form of a servant,
being born in the likeness of men.

Hebrews 4:15–16 (ESV)
For we do not have a high priest
who is unable to sympathize
with our weaknesses,
but one who in every respect
has been tempted as we are, yet without sin.

Let us then with confidence
draw near to the throne of grace,
that we may receive mercy
and find grace to help in time of need.

Psalm 34:18 (ESV)
The LORD is near to the brokenhearted
and saves the crushed in spirit.

Romans 10:8–9 (ESV)
"The word is near you,
in your mouth and in your heart"
(that is, the word of faith that we proclaim);
because, if you confess with your mouth that
Jesus is Lord and believe in your heart
that God raised him from the dead,
you will be saved.

Our Mortal Form, For Mortals' Sake

Just recently, our youngest climbed into bed with us in the middle of the night. He is almost too big for that now; but he had a bad dream, so he wanted to be near mom and dad, where he felt safe and warm and protected and loved. I grieve that one of these nights will be the last time he seeks comfort in snuggles; he's growing up so fast ...

When my father-in-law came home from the hospital for the last time, we put him in his own bedroom, in his own bed. We gathered as family and sang and prayed and kept vigil over those final days of decline. I remember my mother-in-law climbing into bed next to him when he was no longer conscious; snuggling close, embracing his failing body, to let him know even beyond words that he was safe and protected and loved.

When Jesus went to rescue fallen humanity from the sinful mess we had gotten ourselves into, Jesus didn't keep His distance. Jesus came near. We made our bed, and Jesus chose to lie in it with us. Jesus snuggled up close and embraced us, even in our sinful mortality.

Jesus knew hunger, *for you*. Jesus knew thirst, *for you*. Jesus knew exhaustion, *for you*. Jesus knew temptation, *for you*. Jesus knew grief, *for you*. Jesus knew death, *for you*.

It cost Jesus *everything* to draw near to you. He will not turn you away in the night. He will not shun even your deathbed. Jesus is near, holding you in His strong embrace, no matter what.

O love, how deep, how broad, how high,
beyond all thought and fantasy,
that God, the Son of God, should take
our mortal form for mortals' sake!

He sent no angel to our race,
of higher or of lower place,
but wore the robe of human frame,
and to this world Himself He came.

For us baptized, for us He bore
His holy fast and hungered sore;
for us temptation sharp He knew;
for us the tempter overthrew.

For us He prayed; for us He taught;
for us His daily works He wrought,
by words and signs and actions thus
still seeking not Himself, but us.

For us, by wickedness betrayed,
For us, in crown of thorns arrayed,
He bore the shameful cross and death;
for us, He gave His dying breath.

For us He rose from death again;
for us He went on high to reign;
for us He sent His Spirit here
to guide, to strengthen, and to cheer.

All glory to our Lord and God
for love so deep, so high, so broad;
the Trinity whom we adore,
forever and forevermore.

Prayer Experiment: The Ripple Prayer

Write your name in the very center circle on the next page, surrounded by the words, "Jesus is close to ..." In the next ring out, add the people who are closest to you; the family members or friends you see daily or weekly.

In the next ring out, add the names of people who are important to you, but who are more distant relationally; people you don't see on a regular basis.

There is no "wrong answer" when it comes to picking people to pray for today. Invite the Spirit to guide your selection, and don't list more than 5-7 people in each ring. Pray for others next time.

Finally, in the four corners, add the names of people with whom you have a distant or broken relationship, or a relationship strained by hurt or shame. Perhaps there is someone you hardly know at all and you feel guilty about that. If it feels like you have an enemy, put their name down in one of the corners.

Then shade in each of the rings and corners with color as you pray for each person listed, starting with yourself. Use the phrase, "Jesus is close to ..." as a gateway into the next ring.

Jesus is close to people even when they are distant from you, even people who feel like your enemies, people you have hurt or who have hurt you. If you don't know what to pray for someone, simply add color as you hold them before Jesus.

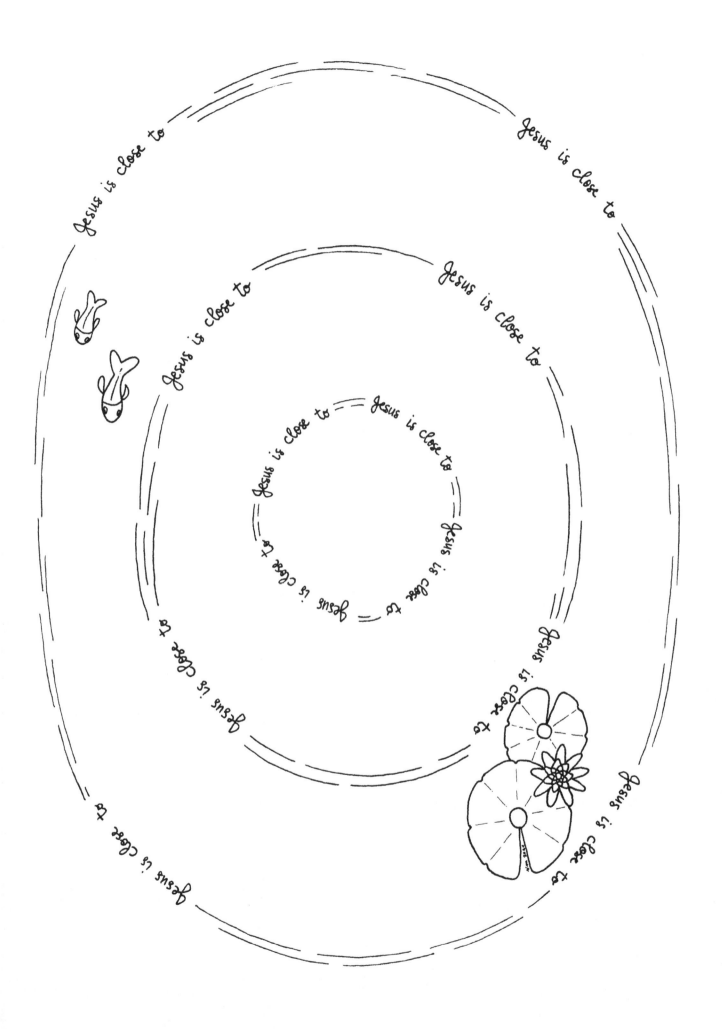

6. How Can I Keep from Singing?

Text and Tune:
Robert Lowry

1. My life flows on in end - less song; A - bove earth's lam - en - ta - tion,
2. Through all the tu - mult and the strife, I hear that mu - sic ring - ing.
3. What though my joys and com - forts die? I know my Sa - vior liv - eth.
4. The peace of Christ makes fresh my heart, A foun - tain ev - er spring - ing!

I catch the sweet, though far off hymn That hails a new cre - a - tion.
It finds an ech - o in my soul. How can I keep from sing - ing?
What though the dark - ness gath-er round? Songs in the night He giv - eth.
All things are mine since I am His! How can I keep from sing - ing?

No storm can shake my in-most calm While to that Rock I'm cling-ing.

Since Christ is Lord of heav'n and earth, How can I keep from sing-ing?

51

John 20:24–29 (ESV)

Now Thomas, one of the twelve, called the Twin, was not with them when Jesus came. So the other disciples told him, "We have seen the Lord."

*But he said to them,
"Unless I see in his hands the mark of the nails, and place my finger into the mark of the nails, and place my hand into his side,*

"I will never believe."

Eight days later, his disciples were inside again, and Thomas was with them. Although the doors were locked, Jesus came and stood among them and said, "Peace be with you."

*Then he said to Thomas,
"Put your finger here, and see my hands; and put out your hand, and place it in my side. Do not disbelieve, but believe."*

Thomas answered him, "My Lord and my God!"

Jesus said to him,

*"Have you believed
   because you have seen me?*

*"Blessed are those who have not seen
   and yet have believed."*

Songs in the Night He Giveth

Call it what you will: pragmatism, realism, skepticism, whatever .... Thomas had it, in spades.

Thomas isn't one to shirk from the cold, hard facts or waste time wishing life were different. In the face of brutally clear evidence that Jesus is dead, Thomas quite pragmatically refuses to believe Jesus is alive again.

Jesus meets "I Refuse to Believe" Thomas there in his unbelief. Jesus makes tangible evidence, His *body*, available for this skeptical, pragmatic realist. And then Jesus proclaims a benediction—not denouncing Thomas so much as encouraging us—"Blessed are those who don't see, and yet believe."

Jesus knows what that's like, to not see and yet to believe. With clear evidence to the contrary, with unnatural darkness blinding His swollen eyes, rough splinters raking His shredded back, and fluid slowly filling His lungs, Jesus chose to entrust His spirit to a Father who was clearly absent. Jesus did not see, and yet He believed.

Oh, so slowly, but Oh, so surely, the Holy Spirit is shaping your skeptical, pragmatic, realist Thomas-heart to be more and more like the heart of the Faithful Son, the Blessed One, who trusted His Father beyond what He could see.

You have blessed moments of trust beyond sight. You know faith, even in your doubt. You sing a New Creation song, even when the night is dark.

NO STORM CAN SHAKE MY INMOST CALM WHILE TO THAT ROCK I'M CLINGING. SINCE CHRIST IS LORD OF HEAVEN & EARTH, HOW CAN I KEEP FROM SINGING?

My life flows on in endless song;
above earth's lamentation,
I catch the sweet, though far off hymn
that hails a new creation.

No storm can shake my inmost calm
while to that Rock I'm clinging.
Since Christ is Lord of heaven and earth,
how can I keep from singing?

Through all the tumult and the strife,
I hear that music ringing.
It finds an echo in my soul.
How can I keep from singing?

What though my joys and comforts die?
I know my Savior liveth.
What though the darkness gather round?
Songs in the night He giveth.

The peace of Christ makes fresh my heart,
a fountain ever springing!
All things are mine since I am His!
How can I keep from singing?

No storm can shake my inmost calm
while to that Rock I'm clinging.
Since Christ is Lord of heaven and earth,
how can I keep from singing?

Faith Experiment: Calm in the Storm

Surrounded by unnatural darkness, the taunts of enemies, and the pain of execution, Jesus cries out to the God who seems so uncaring and far away: "Father, into Your hands I commit my spirit."

That same Jesus, whose trust was vindicated on the third day, now lives and reigns and intercedes for those who find themselves in the dark, in the storm. When God seems uncaring and far away, the Spirit of Jesus shapes the prayer of Jesus on the hearts and lips of those who belong to Jesus.

On the next page you will find a cross, on a rock, in a storm. In the darkness of the thunderclouds and the raging of the sea, write some of the things in your experience that make God seem distant or uncaring. Jesus knows what that's like.

Then, under the cross, safely defended by the Rock, under the protection of the Lord of heaven and earth, write the prayer of trust the Spirit is shaping in you.

Hide yourself in the shelter of the promise: "Blessed are those who have not seen, and yet believe."

> *No storm can shake my inmost calm*
> *while to that Rock I'm clinging.*
> *Since Christ is Lord of heaven and earth,*
> *how can I keep from singing?*

7. In the Cross of Christ I Glory

Text: John Bowring
Tune: Ithamar Conkey

Text and Tune:
Public Domain

Philippians 4:11b–13 (NIV)

*I have learned to
be content
whatever the
circumstances.*

*I know what it is
to be in need,*   *and*   *I know what it is
to have plenty.*

*I have learned
the secret
of being
content
in any
and every
situation,*

*whether
well fed
or hungry,
whether
living
in plenty
or in want.*

*I can do all this
through him
who gives me
strength.*

Bane and Blessing

"Content in all circumstances."

Not, "I like suffering." Not, "I can do whatever I set my mind to." Not, "Don't worry, be happy."

"I have learned the secret of *being content* in any and every situation," Paul says.

What's the secret? What gives you peace when you are in need, as well as when you have plenty? What keeps you from sinful self-reliance when you are well fed, as well as when you are hungry? What makes the ups and down of bane and blessing, pain and pleasure possible to bear?

What's Paul's secret? Paul knows the risen Jesus; that changes everything.

Because you know Jesus, your success and security lead to prayers of thankfulness and dependence. Because you know Jesus, your lack and uncertainty lead to prayers of deep need and dependence.

All the gifts God gives in this present creation you can receive with joy from Jesus, the gift-giver. All the pain you will ever know you will suffer through with Jesus, the burden-sharer.

You *already know* the secret: you share all your griefs and joys with Jesus. And you are *still learning* to live out the secret: little by little doing all things through the One who gives you strength.

The risen Jesus, in all circumstances.

In the cross of Christ I glory,
tow'ring o'er the wrecks of time.
All the light of sacred story
gathers round its head sublime.

When the woes of life o'ertake me,
hopes deceive, and fears annoy,
never shall the cross forsake me;
lo, it glows with peace and joy.

When the sun of bliss is beaming
light and love upon my way,
from the cross the radiance streaming
adds more luster to the day.

Bane and blessing, pain and pleasure
by the Cross are sanctified;
Peace is there that knows no measure,
joys that through all time abide.

Prayer Experiment: The INRI Prayer

Whether your prayer today is focused on joy or sorrow (or a little of both), use the cross on the next page to slow down and focus your time of prayer.

First, pray as you write. Each box in the cross-shaped grid gets a single, capital letter, with no punctuation and no space between words. As you write, use initials for the names of people, for important words, or for sensitive topics.

As you pray, you can choose to include some of the following Latin initials as shorthand.

- SDG: to God alone be the Glory
- JJ: Jesus Help
- DV: God willing
- VDMA: The Word of the Lord endures forever

When you are done, go back and pray a second time as you add color to all of the sets of initials you used. Try to keep a unique color for each set of unique initials.

Finally, pray this prayer a third time as you go back and add color to the rest of the prayer. If you can, use a color different from all the sets of initials.

This INRI Prayer slows you down, keeps your prayer confidential, and allows you to walk through the same prayer three times, all in the shape of the cross of Jesus of Nazareth, King of the Jews.

8. I Am Trusting Thee, Lord Jesus

Text: Frances Havergal
Tune: Henry Baker

Text and Tune:
Public Domain

1. I am trust-ing Thee, Lord Je - sus, Trust - ing on - ly Thee;
2. I am trust-ing Thee for par - don; At Thy feet I bow,
3. I am trust-ing Thee for cleans - ing In the crim - son flood;
4. I am trust-ing Thee to guide me; Thou a - lone shalt lead,
5. I am trust-ing Thee for pow - er; Thine can ne - ver fail.
6. I am trust-ing thee, Lord Jes - us; Ne - ver let me fall.

Trust - ing Thee for full sal - va - tion, Great and free.
For Thy grace and ten - der mer - cy Trust - ing now.
Trust - ing Thee to make me ho - ly By Thy blood.
Ev - ry day and hour sup - ply - ing All my need.
Words which Thou Thy - self shall give me Must pre - vail.
I am trust - ing Thee for - ev - er And for all.

Matthew 6:26–34 (ESV)

Look at the birds of the air:
they neither sow nor reap nor gather into barns,
and yet your heavenly Father feeds them.
Are you not of more value than they?
And which of you by being anxious
can add a single hour to his span of life?

And why are you anxious about clothing?
Consider the lilies of the field, how they grow:
they neither toil nor spin,
yet I tell you, even Solomon in all his glory
was not arrayed like one of these.

But if God so clothes the grass of the field,
which today is alive and
tomorrow is thrown into the oven,
will he not much more clothe you,
O you of little faith?

Therefore do not be anxious, saying,
'What shall we eat?' or 'What shall we drink?'
or 'What shall we wear?' For the Gentiles seek
after all these things, and your heavenly Father
knows that you need them all.

But seek first the kingdom of God
and his righteousness, and all these things
will be added to you.

Therefore do not be anxious about tomorrow, for
tomorrow will be anxious for itself. Sufficient for
the day is its own trouble.

Forever and for All

The birds and flowers don't *try hard* to entrust their lives to God's care; they just do.

They don't really have a choice. But then, maybe we don't really either. We can be anxious about that dependence, but being anxious doesn't help.

So Jesus invites you to trust His heart and His provision for everything you need. Jesus wants you to *know* you receive from His Father everything you have. But more than that, Jesus wants you to *live out* the kind of simple, natural, and complete dependence you see in the birds of the air and the lilies of the field.

Birds don't even recognize their need, yet they live in dependence and trust. You *do* recognize your need—even to the point of *anxiety*—so your dependence can sometimes feel like a threat, and trust can be hard to come by.

You trust Jesus and depend on Jesus for big things like forgiveness, and salvation, and eternal life. That's good. Jesus wants you to need Him for all of that. And then Jesus wants you to translate that trust into the everyday, ordinary, ongoing needs of your daily, human, bodily existence.

You get both: you get to turn to Jesus for your small, personal, daily needs as well as for the big, universal, eternal Kingdom of God. You don't have to *try hard* to entrust your week and your eternity to God's care; just lean into your everyday need, and live a life of dependence. Just like the birds.

I am trusting Thee, Lord Jesus,
trusting only Thee;
trusting Thee for full salvation,
great and free.

I am trusting Thee for pardon;at Thy feet I bow,
for Thy grace and tender mercy
trusting now.

I am trusting Thee for cleansing
in the crimson flood;
trusting Thee to make me holy
by Thy blood.

I am trusting Thee to guide me;
Thou alone shalt lead,
every day and hour supplying
all my need.

I am trusting Thee for power;
Thine can never fail.
words which Thou Thyself shalt give me
must prevail.

I am trusting Thee, Lord Jesus;
never let me fall.
I am trusting Thee forever
and for all.

Faith Experiment: Trust Scenes

The Scriptures invite us into the simple trust shown by animals who aren't working hard at trusting; they just naturally need God to provide.

Choose an animal from one or more of the Bible verses on the following pages. (Or check out Job 39!) Do a little research to learn something about that animal and its habitat. Then do one or both of the following.

1. Grab a 4x6 card (or make your own), draw or cut and paste a picture of your animal. Add facts like their habits and habitat. On the back, write out a Bible verse that connects to your animal and leads you to pray.

2. Sketch the animal you researched in a moment of dependence or rest. Add a Scripture verse as a prayer prompt.

Psalm 104:18

Rock Badger

- aka Syrian Rock Hyrax

- live in crevasses of rocky places

- post a "sentry" to look out for danger while the others find food

- love to sunbathe and spend 95% of their time lying around

- singing – whistles, twitters, shrieks, and squeals – is a favorite pastime

p.maier

the EARTH is full of your creatures...
these ALL look to YOU to give their them food
when you IN DUE SEASON. OPEN YOUR HAND, they are filled with good things.
Psalm 104:24, 27-28

Look at the birds of the air; they do not sow or reap or store away in barns, and yet your heavenly Father feeds them. Are you not much more valuable than they? (Matthew 6:26, NIV)

The wild beasts will honor me, the jackals and the ostriches, for I give water in the wilderness, rivers in the desert, to give drink to my chosen people. (Isaiah 43:20, ESV)

As the deer pants for streams of water, so my soul pants for you, my God. (Psalm 42:1, NIV)

Praise the LORD from the earth, you great sea creatures and all ocean depths. (Psalm 148:7, NIV)

He made my feet like the feet of a deer and set me secure on the heights. (2 Samuel 22:34, ESV)

[The LORD] provides food for the cattle and for the young ravens when they call. (Psalm 147:9, NIV)

Even the sparrow finds a home, and the swallow a nest for herself, where she may lay her young, at your altars, O LORD of hosts, my King and my God. (Psalm 84: 3, ESV)

You make springs gush forth in the valleys; they flow between the hills; they give drink to every beast of the field; the wild donkeys quench their thirst.

Beside them the birds of the heavens dwell; they sing among the branches.

The trees of the LORD are watered abundantly, the cedars of Lebanon that he planted. In them the birds build their nests; the stork has her home in the fir trees.

The high mountains are for the wild goats; the rocks are a refuge for the rock badgers.

You make darkness, and it is night, when all the beasts of the forest creep about. The young lions roar for their prey, seeking their food from God.

O LORD, how manifold are your works!

In wisdom have you made them all; the earth is full of your creatures. Here is the sea, great and wide, which teems with creatures innumerable, living things both small and great.

These all look to you, to give them their food in due season. When you give it to them, they gather it up; when you open your hand, they are filled with good things.

(Psalm 104:10–12; 16–18; 20–21, 24–25; 27–28, ESV)

9. Come Unto Me, Ye Weary

Text: William Dix
Tune: Friedrich Anthes

1. "Come un-to me, ye wea - ry, And I will give you rest."
2. "Come un-to me, ye wan - d'rers, And I will give you light."
3. "Come un-to me, ye faint - ing, And I will give you life."
4. "And who - ev - er com - eth, I will not cast him out."

O bless - ed voice of Je - sus, Which comes to hearts op - pressed!
O lov - ing voice of Je - sus, Which comes to cheer the night!
O cheer - ing voice of Je - sus, Which comes to aid our strife!
O pa - tient love of Je - sus, Which drives a - way our doubt,

It tells of ben - e - dic - tion, Of par - don, grace, and peace,
Our hearts were filled with sad - ness, And we had lost our way;
The foe is stern and ea - ger, The fight is fierce and long;
Which, though we be un-worth - y Of love so great and free,

Of joy that has no end - ing, Of love that can - not cease.
But Thou have brought us glad - ness And songs at break of day.
But Thou hast made us might - y And strong - er than the strong.
In - vites us ver - y sin - ners To come, dear Lord, to Thee!

83

Come unto Me ye weary and I will give you Rest

R Helmreich 2020

Psalm 127:2 (NIV)
[The LORD] grants sleep to those he loves.

Matthew 8:24–26 (NIV)
Suddenly a furious storm came up on the lake, so that the waves swept over the boat.

But Jesus was sleeping.

The disciples went and woke him, saying, "Lord, save us! We're going to drown!"

He replied, "You of little faith, why are you so afraid?"

Then he got up and rebuked the winds and the waves, and it was completely calm.

Matthew 11:27–30 (ESV)
[Jesus declared:] "All things have been handed over to me by my Father, and no one knows the Son except the Father, and no one knows the Father except the Son and anyone to whom the Son chooses to reveal him.

Come to me, all who labor and are heavy laden, and I will give you rest.

Take my yoke upon you, and learn from me, for I am gentle and lowly in heart, and you will find rest for your souls.

For my yoke is easy, and my burden is light."

I Will Give You Rest

Sleep is an act of trust. Sleep means you have relinquished control of your surroundings, and it's going to be OK.

Sleep is a gift from God. Sleep brings refreshing renewal while you are helpless and vulnerable. Only the confident can rest secure.

We find Jesus asleep on a cushion in a boat, and when a sudden storm gets so violent that even career fishermen are shaking from fear, Jesus sleeps on.

Yes, Jesus was fully human and exhausted. But more than that, Jesus entrusted His life and His situation to His Heavenly Father. Jesus could sleep securely in the midst of the storm because He knew the One who holds the power of the wind and waves.

When Jesus finally does wake up, His response is not, "Whoa! Look at the storm!! You should have gotten me sooner!" Instead, in the midst of that fearful gale, Jesus asks, "Where is your faith?"

Sleep is a gift from God. Sleep is an act of trust. You can sleep securely, like Jesus in the storm, because your Heavenly Father is still in control, even when you are not.

Sleep well.

"Come unto Me, ye weary, and I will give you rest."
Oh blessed voice of Jesus,
which comes to hearts oppressed!
It tells of benediction,
of pardon, grace, and peace,
of joy that hath no ending,
of love that cannot cease.

"Come unto Me, ye wand'rers, and I will give you light."
Oh loving voice of Jesus,
which comes to cheer the night!
Our hearts were filled with sadness,
and we had lost our way;
But Thou hast brought us gladness
and songs at break of day.

"Come unto Me, ye fainting, and I will give you life."
Oh cheering voice of Jesus,
which comes to aid our strife!
The foe is stern and eager,
the fight is fierce and long;
but Thou hast made us mighty
and stronger than the strong.

"And whosoever cometh, I will not cast him out."
Oh patient love of Jesus,
which drives away our doubt;
which, though we be unworthy
of love so great and free,
invites us very sinners
to come, dear Lord, to Thee!

Prayer Experiment: The Lord's Rest

I know sleep is a loving gift from God, but I don't always receive that gift very well. Sometimes anxiety or excitement keep my mind racing. Sometimes burdens or grief have me staring at the ceiling in the middle of the night. Sometimes my need to *do* something, anything, outweighs my need for rest.

I find if I *try hard* to fall asleep, I'll keep tossing and turning. What does help, at least sometimes, is not working hard to sleep, but receiving that awake time as an invitation to prayer.

Of course, all of the things swirling in my head and keeping me awake can be a prayer list of sorts. But after the first round, even praying about that to-do list can raise my anxiety or make me think of one more detail that needs my attention.

So I usually resort to saying the Lord's Prayer over and over, slowly, and with intention. Jesus gave us that prayer. Jesus invites us into that prayer. Jesus invites us into the simple trust that can sleep in confidence, even when there is so much to do.

On the next page, below the image of Jesus asleep in a boat, write out the Lord's Prayer slowly and with intention. Use that prayer time to quiet your heart and mind. Give over your worries and anxieties. Submit your need to be active to God's will for you to rest in confidence. Deep breath. You are not in control. And it's going to be OK.

10. Come, Thou Fount of Every Blessing

Text: Robert Robinson
Tune: Unknown

Text and Tune:
Public Domain

1. Come, Thou Fount of ev'-ry bless-ing, Tune my heart to sing Thy grace;
2. Here I raise my Eb-en-e-zer, Hith-er by Thy help I've come;
3. Oh, to grace how great a debt-or Dai-ly I'm con-strained to be;
4. Oh, that day when freed from sin-ning, I shall see Thy love-ly face;

Streams of mer-cy, nev-er ceas-ing, Call for songs of loud-est praise.
And I hope, by Thy good plea-sure, Safe-ly to ar-rive at home.
Let that grace now like a fet-ter Bind my wan-d'ring heart to Thee:
Clothed then in the blood-washed lin-en, how I'll sing Thy won-drous grace!

While the hope of end-less glo-ry Fills my heart with joy and love,
Je-sus sought me when a strang-er, Wan-d'ring from the fold of God;
Prone to wan-der, Lord, I feel it; Prone to leave the God I love.
Come, my Lord, no long-er tar-ry; Take my ran-som'd soul a-way;

Teach me ev-er to a-dore Thee; May I still Thy good-ness prove.
He, to res-cue me from dan-ger, In-ter-posed His pre-cious blood.
Here's my heart, oh take and seal it, Seal it for Thy courts a-bove.
Send Thine an-gels soon to car-ry me to realms of end-less day.

1 Samuel 7:6–12 (NIV)

On that day they fasted and there they confessed, "We have sinned against the LORD." Now Samuel was serving as leader of Israel at Mizpah.

When the Philistines heard that Israel had assembled at Mizpah, the rulers of the Philistines came up to attack them. When the Israelites heard of it, they were afraid because of the Philistines. They said to Samuel, "Do not stop crying out to the LORD our God for us, that he may rescue us from the hand of the Philistines."

Then Samuel took a suckling lamb and sacrificed it as a whole burnt offering to the LORD. He cried out to the LORD on Israel's behalf, and the LORD answered him.

While Samuel was sacrificing the burnt offering, the Philistines drew near to engage Israel in battle. But that day the LORD thundered with loud thunder against the Philistines and threw them into such a panic that they were routed before the Israelites. The men of Israel rushed out of Mizpah and pursued the Philistines, slaughtering them along the way to a point below Beth Kar. Then Samuel took a stone and set it up between Mizpah and Shen.

He named it Ebenezer [Stone of Help], saying, "Thus far the LORD has helped us."

Here I Raise My Ebenezer

The day started in repentance, with fasting and confession, with sacrifice and absolution. God's people wanted to return with their whole hearts, and God's prophet helped bring them back into relationship with the God they had abandoned.

The day ended in a military victory against superior occupation forces; a victory that clearly and unquestionably came from God's own hand.

To remind God's people of that day—perhaps more, to remind God's people of God's mercy and faithfulness and power—the prophet sets up a memorial stone. Eben-Ezer; "Stone of Help."

Like a milepost, it signifies the distance God covered to save people who didn't deserve it. Like a historical marker, it points to great events that took place on this very spot. Like a tombstone, it recalls the life and actions of a Real Person. Everyone who passed that Stone would know: my God lives and has done great things for me!

You could raise an Eben-Ezer, too. God has brought you this far by faith, and God will keep acting in grace to bring you home. You have mileposts, bread and wine, that show you how far your God has come to save you. You have historical markers, God's Word of Life active on this very spot. But most of all, you have a tombstone, a Stone of Help rolled away from the empty grave of Jesus, that promises your tombstone will also one day be obsolete.

My God lives and has done great things for me!

Come, Thou fount of ev'ry blessing,
tune my heart to sing Thy grace;
streams of mercy, never ceasing,
call for songs of loudest praise.
While the hope of endless glory
fills my heart with joy and love,
teach me ever to adore Thee;
may I still Thy goodness prove.

Here I raise my Ebenezer,
hither by Thy help I've come;
and I hope, by Thy good pleasure,
safely to arrive at home.
Jesus sought me when a stranger,
wand'ring from the fold of God;
He, to rescue me from danger,
interposed His precious blood.

Oh, to grace how great a debtor
daily I'm constrained to be;
let that grace now, like a fetter
bind my wand'ring heart to Thee:
prone to wander, Lord, I feel it;
prone to leave the God I love.
Here's my heart, Oh take and seal it,
seal it for Thy courts above.

Oh, that day when freed from sinning,
I shall see Thy lovely face;
clothed then in the bloodwashed linen,
how I'll sing Thy wondrous grace!
Come, my Lord, no longer tarry;
take my ransom'd soul away;
send Thine angels soon to carry
me to realms of endless day.

Faith Experiment: Rock of Help

Eben-Ezer, the Stone of Help, stood as a reminder of God's action and God's mercy. If you were to raise your own Eben-Ezer, what events in your life might fit on your memorial Stone of Help?

Think of a time in your life when God acted in mercy to bring you help. What was the danger? What help did you need? What did God do? What was the result?

On the large Stone of Help on the next page, briefly sketch four main themes from a story of God's help in your life. Think of this as a storyboard: the drawing can be rough (use stick figures if you want!); just capture the basic flow of the action.

The first scene should show where you were or what you were doing when it all started. The second should try and capture what went terribly wrong; why you needed help, what the need or danger was.

Then, in the third scene, sketch God's faithful action in your life. What brought resolution to your conflict and how was Jesus present and involved?

In the final scene, show the situation that resulted from God's action. What was life like after that?

When you have sketched four scenes from an event in your life that shows God's help, share your Eben-Ezer with a friend or family member. Use your Stone of Help to tell the story. It will build your faith, and theirs.

11. O God, Our Help in Ages Past

Text: Isaac Watts
Tune: William Croft

Text and Tune:
Public Domain

Psalm 22:1–5, 10–11, 30–31 (NIV)

My God, my God, why have you forsaken me?
Why are you so far from saving me,
so far from my cries of anguish?

My God, I cry out by day, but you do not answer,
by night, but I find no rest.

Yet you are enthroned as the Holy One;
you are the one Israel praises.

In you our ancestors put their trust;
they trusted and you delivered them.

To you they cried out and were saved;
in you they trusted and were not put to shame.

From birth I was cast on you;
from my mother's womb you have been my God.

Do not be far from me, for trouble is near and
there is no one to help.

Posterity will serve him;
future generations will be told about the LORD.

They will proclaim his righteousness,
declaring to a people yet unborn:

He has done it!

Our Hope for Years to Come

In excruciating pain, close to death, King Jesus echoes the words of King David, words that hold onto God's faithful action in the past as well as God's faithful promise for the future.

In the moment, both David and Jesus speak of separation from God; the first king in his sin, the second in His innocence. There, on the cross, Jesus experiences the full abandonment of God, complete separation from the Father, in a way that you and I, by God's grace, never will.

But even that prayer of abandonment turns to God's action in the past and God's promise for the future to invite and invoke God's presence in the present. "*Our ancestors* put their trust in You, and You delivered them," prays the king in a moment of pain and confusion and loneliness. "*And future generations* will declare Your righteous actions."

Past. And future. And I need You, *right now.*

You have a God who has been faithful in the past, in *your* past. You have a God who has made faithful promises for the future, for *your* future. You have a God who is there for you in the midst of your present, even when your God feels far away.

Jesus does not get an immediate answer to His prayer. Jesus has to walk through death before God finally saves and vindicates and glorifies Him. But in the present, Jesus entrusts His future to the faithful God of His past.

And so do we.

faithful GOD "He has done it." Psalm 22:31

HOPE for years to come....

p. maier

O God, our help in ages past,
our hope for years to come,
our shelter from the stormy blast,
and our eternal home:

Under the shadow of Thy throne
Thy saints have dwelt secure;
sufficient is Thine arm alone,
and our defense is sure.

Before the hills in order stood
or earth received her frame,
from everlasting Thou art God,
to endless years the same.

A thousand ages in Thy sight
are like an evening gone,
short as the watch that ends the night
before the rising sun.

Time, like an ever-rolling stream,
soon bears us all away;
we fly forgotten as a dream
dies at the op'ning day.

O God, our help in ages past,
our hope for years to come,
still be our guard while troubles last
and our eternal home!

Return, O God of love, return;
Earth is a tiresome place:
how long shall we Thy children mourn
our absence from Thy face?

Thy wonders to Thy servants show,
make Thine own work complete;
then shall our souls Thy glory know,
and own Thy love was great.

Then shall we shine before Thy throne
in all Thy beauty, Lord:
and the poor service we have done
meet a divine reward.

Prayer Experiment: The Triptych Prayer

A "triptych" is a piece of art that hangs above an altar in a sanctuary and tells a story in three panels.

In the left panel of the triptych on the next page, repeat the story of God's faithful action in the past from your Rock of Help in Chapter 10. Then add color to the scene of God's faithful action in the future on the right panel.

Finally, in the center panel, write or sketch your present prayer requests. Borrow words or phrases from Psalm 22 or from the hymn. Lay your present concerns before Jesus in light of God's faithful action in the past and God's faithful promise for the future.

12. It is Well With My Soul

Text: Horatio Spafford
Tune: Philip Bliss

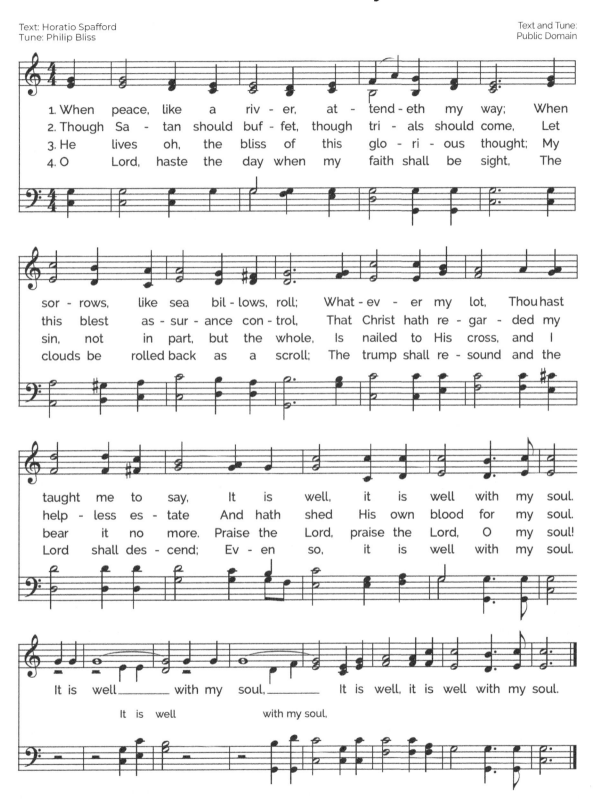

1. When peace, like a riv - er, at - tend - eth my way; When
2. Though Sa - tan should buf - fet, though tri - als should come, Let
3. He lives oh, the bliss of this glo - ri - ous thought; My
4. O Lord, haste the day when my faith shall be sight, The

sor - rows, like sea bil - lows, roll; What - ev - er my lot, Thou hast
this blest as - sur - ance con - trol, That Christ hath re - gar - ded my
sin, not in part, but the whole, Is nailed to His cross, and I
clouds be rolled back as a scroll; The trump shall re - sound and the

taught me to say, It is well, it is well with my soul.
help - less es - tate And hath shed His own blood for my soul.
bear it no more. Praise the Lord, praise the Lord, O my soul!
Lord shall des - cend; Ev - en so, it is well with my soul.

It is well_____ with my soul,_____ It is well, it is well with my soul.

It is well with my soul,

1 Corinthians 13:8–13 (ESV)

Love never ends.

As for prophecies, they will pass away;
as for tongues, they will cease;
as for knowledge, it will pass away.

For we know in part
and we prophesy in part,
but when [completeness] comes,
the partial will pass away.

When I was a child,
I spoke like a child,
I thought like a child,
I reasoned like a child.

When I became a man,
I gave up childish ways.

For now we see in a mirror dimly,
but then face to face.

Now I know in part;
then I shall know fully,
even as I have been fully known.

So now faith, hope, and love abide, these three;
but the greatest of these is love.

When My Faith Shall Be Sight

If Paul asked you which is the greatest, (A) faith; (B) hope; or (C) love, which one would you choose?

I would go with (D) all of the above. Except that's not an option. So I think I would probably go with (A) faith.

You know, *faith*? As in, "We walk by *faith* and not by sight?" "We are justified by *faith* apart from works of the law?" "Go in peace, your *faith* has saved you?"

And I would get the multiple choice quiz wrong. Paul's answer is Love. Why? *Love never ends.*

You see, faith and hope are temporary. Faith and hope give us access to what we *can't see*. Until we *can* see it, that is; then we won't need faith or hope.

Trust that the time will come when you will no longer need trust. Long and hope for the time when longing and hope will be fulfilled.

Rejoice that you catch a glimpse, already now, by faith, of who Jesus is and what Jesus is doing; and rejoice that one day you will exchange these eyes of faith—blurry eyes that can just barely recognize movement in the dim reflection of a dull metal mirror—with clear and perfect New Creation eyes, eyes that will see Jesus face to face.

You desperately need faith. But only until you have Love by sight. Love never ends.

When peace like a river attendeth my way,
when sorrows like sea billows roll;
whatever my lot, Thou hast taught me to say,
"It is well, it is well with my soul."

It is well with my soul; it is well, it is well with my soul.

Though Satan should buffet, though trials should come,
let this blest assurance control:
that Christ hath regarded my helpless estate,
and hath shed His own blood for my soul.

It is well with my soul; it is well, it is well with my soul.

He lives—oh, the bliss of this glorious thought!
—my sin, not in part, but the whole,
is nailed to the cross, and I bear it no more;
praise the Lord, praise the Lord, O my soul!

It is well with my soul; it is well, it is well with my soul.

O Lord, haste the day when my faith shall be sight,
the clouds be rolled back as a scroll;
the trump shall resound and the Lord shall descend;
even so, it is well with my soul.

It is well with my soul; it is well, it is well with my soul.

Faith Experiment: Faith, Hope, and Love

Use a variety of colors, letter sizes, and script styles to write inside the words on the next page.

Inside the word "Faith" make a list of things that encourage, strengthen, feed, or empower your trust in Jesus, even when you can't see Him clearly. Quote Bible verses. Add the names of people. List ways your faith is strengthened. Capture elements of your life that strengthen and encourage your faith.

Inside the word "Hope" make a similar list, but this time focus on promises you look forward to being fulfilled. Add Scripture that inspires longing and expectation in you. Write out some of the promises from Jesus you know you can trust. Where does your hope come from?

Finally, inside the word "Love" write about things that you know will endure forever; love never ends. What realities do you have now by faith that you will have then by sight? What is the object of your hope? What verses give you a glimpse of what will you see clearly when you see face to face?

Faith, hope, and love: these three abide; but the greatest of these is love.

What's Your Next Step?

We hope this Hymn Journal has been a useful tool as you seek to get to know Jesus better. Being intentional about your faith isn't easy: keep it up!

As you try to take a next step following Jesus, we have found that having a regular time with a regular person or two is a real help. Get together a couple times a month, invite the Spirit to be present, and simply talk about these three questions:

- What's Jesus speaking into your life?
- What response is Jesus shaping in you?
- What promise from Jesus is guiding your next step?

If you don't know how to begin to answer one of those questions, that's an invitation from Jesus to turn to Him again in need.

Your next step might be, "Talk to someone about figuring out my next step." Maybe your prayer is, "Jesus, I have no idea what I am supposed to be doing right now." Or simply, "Jesus, help!"

Needing Jesus is the single most important trait of any disciple. He won't give up on you.

For the Record

Look back over the work you have done in this Hymn Journal. Where have you grown? What have you learned? What was meaningful to you? What was interesting or confusing or helpful or frustrating? What emotions did you experience as you walked through this book?

If you find a common theme, you could wonder with Jesus what He is up to in your life. But whether you have a clear direction for a next step or only a vague inkling, try to put something down in each of the following areas.

If you get stuck, phone a friend. If you just don't know, let that open question be your next step. Jesus is with you, no matter what.

Because I like being intentional in my faith walk, I'm looking for what Jesus is inviting me into next. After prayerful conversation, here is

My Next Step:

Because I know we follow Jesus better when we follow Him together, I'm going to invite a couple of people to walk with me for a ways on this faith journey. So I'll take this next step

With These People:

Because I know I am not up for this journey on my own, and because I want to learn more and more how to depend on Jesus in my everyday life, I am consciously holding on to

This Promise from Jesus that Guides My Next Step:

Something to Share

We follow Jesus better when we follow Him together. That means we all have something to learn, and something to share.

Find one thing that made a difference in your faith or life as you have experienced this Hymn Journal. Now share that experience with a friend.

Maybe it was a visual faith experiment or a particular hymn verse. Maybe it was a specific thought or Scripture reading. Maybe the time you set aside in God's presence helped you see something you had forgotten or had never seen before.

Take one thing—any one thought, or drawing, or reading, or hymn—that had an impact on you, and share it with someone else. Try to express why it was meaningful for you. Invite them to run an experiment and see if it might be meaningful for them, too.

By sharing even one thing with someone else, you plant that Word deeper in your own heart and life. You also extend an invitation for someone else to begin to wonder what Jesus is up to in their life.

Following Jesus can be scary and exciting and difficult and rewarding; and it's just more fun when you share the experience with others.

We follow Jesus better when we follow Him together. Thanks for sharing this leg of the journey with us; may Jesus guide and bless your next step on this adventure of faith!

What I shared:

Who I shared it with:

How it went:

The INRI Prayer

The Big Rocks Prayer

About Visual Faith Ministry

Visual Faith Ministry is the collaborative effort of online and "in-real-life" learning communities to enrich, encourage and enable the vital connections between visual and kinesthetic learning styles and the storytelling of God's faithfulness in our lives.

Visual Faith is all about reading, reflecting, and responding to God's Word. It welcomes writing, drawing, designs, and color to create reminders of faith that help tell the story for followers of Jesus. Visual Faith reminds us that we are made in the image of a creative God.

Visual Faith honors God's creative sanctification of believers on a daily basis and is the basic process of bringing together our great gifts of prayer and God's Word. It adds visual, kinesthetic, and tactile adaptations that make meaning for us in our daily lives. Visual Faith is a "selfie" of our time with God, helping us to remember, retain, and be ready to share it with others.

In all of these ways and more, Visual Faith helps to answer the question, "What does this mean for me?"

Find more Visual Faith resources at
www.visualfaithmin.org

VISUAL
FAITH™
MINISTRY
TELLING THE STORY OF HIS FAITHFULNESS

About Valerie Matyas

Valerie Matyas is a Visual Faith Coach and the Educational Development Consultant for Visual Faith Ministry.

Valerie is a sought-after speaker for retreats, conferences, and workshops. She enjoys presenting visual faith practices to professional church workers and lay people of all ages.

Valerie served as the Lead Illustrator for the hymn journals *When from Death I'm Free* and *Ponder Anew* as well as providing illustrations for the following:

Praise to the Lord, the Almighty
O Love, How Deep, How Broad, How High

Valerie lives in Michigan with her clerical-wearing husband and four young children.

Meet the Visual Faith Illustrators

Emily Adams
What a Friend We Have in Jesus;
Great is Thy Faithfulness

Emily is a visual faith artist and contributor to the Visual Church Year Project. She loves Bible Journaling and using art to make deep and lasting connections to God's Word. Emily lives in Oregon and is a pastor's wife and stay-at-home mom to two young children.

Ann Gillaspie
How Firm a Foundation;
Come, Thou Fount of Every Blessing

Ann Gillaspie is a Visual Faith Coach and regular contributor to the Visual Church Year Project. She specializes in hand lettering and enjoys bringing her love for art and faith together as a means to worship God. Ann is a pastor's wife, mom of two grown sons and daughters-in-law, and grandma to two little boys and a little girl.

Katie Helmreich

In the Cross of Christ I Glory;
Come unto Me, Ye Weary

Katie Helmreich is an artist and illustrator, and regularly contributes to the Visual Church Year Project and other Visual Faith resources. She enjoys teaching Visual Faith art classes regularly helping others grow and share in the joy of this experience. Katie lives in Michigan with her engineer and firefighter husband and three kids.

Karen Hunter

How Can I Keep from Singing;
It is Well with My Soul

Karen Hunter is a visual faith artist and regular contributor to the Visual Church Year Project and multiple online Visual Faith forums. She loves spending time in the Word and incorporating a variety of visual faith art into her Bible, journals and faith planner. Karen is a wife, mom, former classroom teacher, and Bible Study leader in her home church in Virginia.

Pat Maier
I Am Trusting Thee, Lord Jesus;
O God, Our Help in Ages Past

Pat Maier is a visual faith artist and co-founder of Visual Faith Ministry. She believes that the creative use of language and art—when connected with God's Word—can touch the heart, promote understanding, and bring joy and connection.

Pat teaches and creates resources for visual processing and was an illustrator for *The Enduring Word Bible*. A retired educator, Pat lives in Michigan where she is most importantly a wife, mother, and grandmother.

About Justin Rossow

Rev. Dr. Justin Rossow preaches, teaches, presents, and writes at the intersection of Scripture, culture, and metaphor theory.

With 20 years of ministry experience focused especially on discipleship, Justin brings a refreshing and encouraging voice to the adventure of helping people delight in taking a next step.

Justin is known for his insight and energy, and writes like he talks: with humor, humility, and profound dependence on Jesus.

Justin and his wife Miriam live in Michigan with their four children.

He is the founder of Next Step Press and The Next Step Community.

Also from Justin Rossow and Next Step Press:

You, Follow Me: A Daily Discipleship Travel Log for Advent and Christmas

When from Death I'm Free: A Hymn Journal for Holy Week

Preaching Metaphor: How to Shape Sermons that Shape People

Delight! Discipleship as the Adventure of Loving and Being Loved (forthcoming)

About Next Step Press

You're trying to follow Jesus; that's awesome!

We want to help.

Next Step Press is a ministry devoted to producing engaging resources that help you delight in taking a next step following Jesus.

When you need to find your path forward, either as an individual or in a small group, we're there for you. One size does not fit all when it comes to discipleship; find something that works for you.

When the task of leading a group feels overwhelming, we can help with that, too. Everything we design for congregations and leaders will support your effort to build and sustain a culture of discipleship, no matter the size of your community. From books, to sermon series, to staff training, to weekend retreats, we've got your back.

We know it's not easy to follow Jesus, and the Next Step Press team wants to alleviate the burden of being a Christian with the joy of being a follower.

What's your next step?

Find out more at
www.FindMyNextStep.org

The Next Step Community

The Next Step Community is a group of people, like you, who need other people to help them take a next step following Jesus.

You won't find any preconceived notions or quick fixes here; just real people trying to follow Jesus in real life. You are welcome to join in!

We follow Jesus better when we follow Him together, so we invite you to share what you experienced in this Hymn Journal by emailing Curator@FindMyNextStep.org.

What experiments helped and why?

Did you customize anything or try a variation that seemed to work for you?

What did you share with someone else, and how did it go?

When you share your story of taking a next step, you help someone else take theirs.

Come, join the community at
community.FindMyNextStep.org

SDG

Made in the USA
Monee, IL
29 May 2020